W9-CSQ-211

Nunavut

Linda Aspen-Baxter

WEIGL EDUCATIONAL PUBLISHERS

Published by Weigl Educational Publishers Limited
6325 10 Street SE
Calgary, Alberta, Canada
T2H 2Z9
Web site: www.weigl.com

We acknowledge the financial support of the Government of Canada through the Book Publishing
Industry Development Program (BPIDP) for our publishing activities.

National Library of Canada Cataloguing in Publication Data
Aspen-Baxter, Linda, 1957-
  Nunavut / Linda Aspen-Baxter.
  (Canadian sites and symbols)
  Includes index.
  ISBN 1-55388-025-0
  1. Provincial emblems--Nunavut--Juvenile literature.
  2. Heraldry--Nunavut--Juvenile literature. I. Title.
  II. Series.
CR213.N85A86 2003   j929.6'09719'5   C2003-910533-4

Printed in the United States of America
1 2 3 4 5 6 7 8 9 0   07 06 05 04 03

Project Coordinator: Donald Wells
Design: Janine Vangool
Layout: Virginia Boulay
Copy Editor: Tina Schwartzenberger
Photo Researcher: Ellen Bryan

Photograph Credits
Every reasonable effort has been made to trace ownership and to obtain permission to reprint
copyright material. The publishers would be pleased to have any errors or omissions brought to
their attention so that they may be corrected in subsequent printings.

Cover: polar bear (**Corel Corporation**); **Corel Corporation**: pages 3T, 3M, 3B, 4, 9, 12, 13T, 18, 20, 21B,
22; **Government of Nunavut**: pages 1, 8; **Lyn Hancock**: pages 5, 6, 7T, 7B, 11T, 11B, 14, 15T, 15B, 16, 17T,
17B, 21T, 23; **Ray Joubert**: page 10; **Courtesy of the Legislative Assembly of Nunavut**: page 19; **Tom
Stack & Associates**: page 13B (**Thomas Kitchin**).

Contents

Introduction   4

What's in a Name?   6

Coat of Arms Closeup   8

Flying the Flag   10

Furry and Feathered Feet   12

Arctic Plants   14

Emblems of the Earth   16

A Symbolic Staff   18

Special Places   20

Quiz   22

Glossary/Index   24

Introduction

Canada is a large country. The ten Canadian provinces and three territories cover a vast amount of land. From one province or territory to another, the people, lifestyles, land, and animals are quite different. Each province and territory has its own **identity**. The provinces and territories use **symbols** to represent this identity. This book looks at the symbols that represent the territory of Nunavut.

Yukon Territory

Northwest Territories

Nunavut

British Columbia

Alberta

Manitoba

Saskatchewan

Nunavut is the most sparsely populated area in Canada.

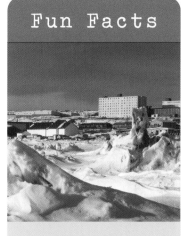

Nunavut became Canada's youngest territory on April 1, 1999. It borders the Northwest Territories on the west and stretches east to Baffin Island and north to Ellesmere Island. People in Nunavut say they live "North of 60" because the territory's southern border lies at 60 degrees north **latitude**. Nunavut's landscape is mostly **tundra**, lakes, mountains, and rocky coastline. Nunavut's official symbols represent its natural beauty and resources.

Nunavut's capital is Iqaluit. Iqaluit is located on Baffin Island.

Nunavut covers more than 2 million square kilometres (772,000 square miles). It has 12 of Canada's 20 largest islands.

Covering about one-fifth of Canada, Nunavut is larger than any other province or territory.

Newfoundland and Labrador

Quebec

Prince Edward Island

New Brunswick

Nova Scotia

Ontario

0	Kilometres	500
0	Miles	310.69

N

What's in a Name?

Nunavut means "our land" in Inuktitut, the language spoken by the Inuit who make up most of the population of the territory. Nunavut is the name of the central and eastern Arctic Inuit's **traditional** home. The Inuit people have lived in this part of Canada for thousands of years. The Inuit were once called *Eskimo*. Now they are called Inuit, which means "people." Although Inuktitut is the Inuit language, many Inuit in western Nunavut speak English. The Inuit language is more common in eastern Nunavut.

The Inuit write their language using symbols. This form of writing was developed by Edmund Peck in 1894.

Arctic Circle
Cercle Arctique   66° 30' N
ᐅᑉ ᐱᐅᑲᑐᓕ ᑭᒻ ᒍᐊᑭ ᒪ

The Inuit people worked with the Government of Canada from 1976 to 1992 to reach an agreement about the new territory. In 1982, the people of the Northwest Territories were asked to vote on whether their territory should be split into two parts. The residents agreed that the Northwest Territories should become two territories. In 1993, after years of negotiation, a land claim agreement was signed. The agreement gave the Inuit control over 351,000 square kilometres (136,000 square miles) of Nunavut. The Inuit people were also granted the fishing, hunting, and mining rights for the territory. On April 1, 1999, Nunavut became an official territory.

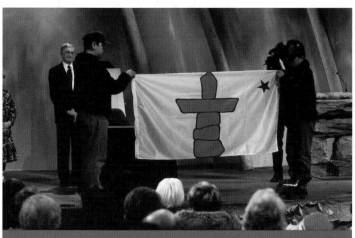

July 9th is officially recognized as Nunavut Day. Everyone who works for the Government of Nunavut has a holiday on Nunavut Day.

Fun Facts

Nunavut uses the same polar bear-shaped license plate as the Northwest Territories.

In 2001, about 27,000 people lived in Nunavut. Eighty-five percent of the population is Inuit.

There are 26 communities in Nunavut.

In many Arctic communities, snow lasts well into June. Sea ice and lake ice remain even longer.

Coat of Arms Closeup

A coat of arms is a special design that represents a group or region. Every Canadian province and territory has its own coat of arms. Nunavut's coat of arms honours the territory's Inuit **heritage**. Each part of the design symbolizes something special about life in this territory.

Fun Facts

Nunavut's coat of arms is known officially as The Arms of Her Majesty in Right of Nunavut. The right to use the coat of arms was granted by Roméo Leblanc, Governor-General of Canada, on March 31, 1999, one day before Nunavut became an official territory.

Features

An igloo, a traditional Inuit winter shelter, is above the shield. It represents the Inuit's traditional way of life.

The caribou stands on one side of the coat of arms.

The gold star is *Niqirtsuituq*, or the North Star. The star represents how the elders guide the people.

Five gold circles sit on top of the shield. They represent the life-giving properties of the Sun.

The colours blue and gold represent the riches of the land, ocean, and sky.

There is an *inukshuk* at the base of the round shield. These human-like stone figures guide people on land and mark special places.

Beside the inukshuk, there is a *qulliq*, or Inuit stone lamp. It stands for light and the warmth of family and community.

Along the base is Nunavut's motto *Nunavut Sanginivut*, or "Nunavut, Our Strength." The motto is written in Inuktitut.

Flying the Flag

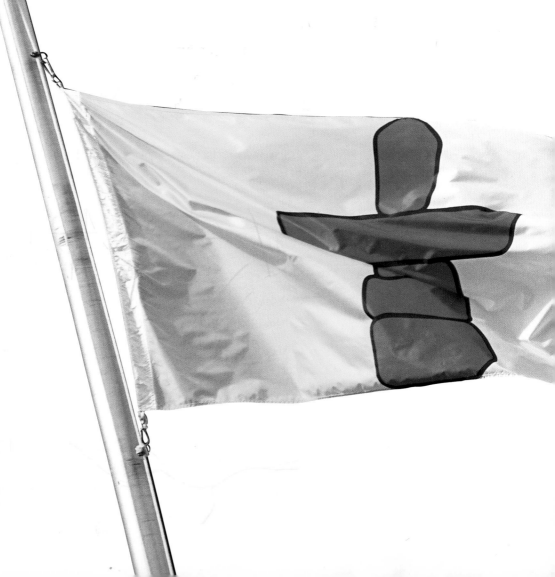

Nunavut's official flag was unveiled on April 1, 1999. People across Canada were invited to submit design ideas for the flag. A special selection committee of elders and artists analyzed the submissions and selected ten finalists for the flag. The flag was designed using the elements and colours from each finalist that best represented the character of Nunavut.

Fun Facts

Icecaps and glaciers cover about 150,000 square kilometres (58,000 square miles) of Nunavut.

Nunavut's frozen lakes are used as roads in winter.

An inukshuk stands in the centre of Nunavut's flag. Niqirtsuituq, or the North Star, is in the top outside corner of the flag. The North Star and the inukshuk were chosen because they have guided the Inuit people across the frozen trails of their homeland for centuries. The North Star also represents the leadership of community elders. The red colour of the inukshuk shows Nunavut's connection to Canada. The colours of blue and gold on the flag symbolize the riches of the land, the sea, and the sky.

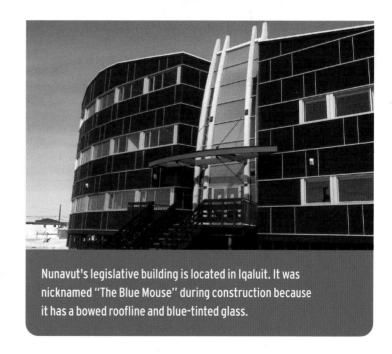

Nunavut's legislative building is located in Iqaluit. It was nicknamed "The Blue Mouse" during construction because it has a bowed roofline and blue-tinted glass.

Furry and Feathered Feet

Many animals live in Nunavut. Caribou and muskox live on the tundra. Polar bears feed on the seals that live along the coast. Many small animals, such as foxes, hares, squirrels, weasels, and wolverines, also live in Nunavut all year. Beluga whales and **narwhals** are found in the Arctic waters off Nunavut's coast. Approximately 230 species of birds live in Nunavut during the summer months. Many of these animals have been important to the Inuit's survival in the Arctic, but it is the *qimmiq*, or the Canadian Inuit dog, that is Nunavut's official animal.

Canadian Inuit dogs have provided transportation in the Arctic for thousands of years.

The Canadian Inuit dog was chosen to be the official animal because it is important to Inuit survival. The qimmiq pulls sleds, helps hunters find seal breathing holes in the ice, and protects the Inuit from muskox and polar bears. The Canadian Inuit dog has a long outer coat and thick undercoat. Even its feet are covered with thick fur.

The rock ptarmigan, Nunavut's official bird, lives in the territory all year. Rock ptarmigans have thick feathers on the tops and bottoms of their feet. The feathers keep their feet warm. Long claws on their feet help them move without slipping on ice.

Adult rock ptarmigans eat plants. Rock ptarmigan chicks eat insects, spiders, and snails.

Fun Facts

About half of the world's polar bears live in Nunavut.

The most luxurious and expensive natural fibers in the world, called *qiviut*, come from the fine under-hair of the muskox.

More than 750,000 caribou live in Nunavut. Their meat and hides have always been important to the Inuit.

Arctic Plants

In Nunavut, the weather is very cold for much of the year, and the ground is permanently frozen. In summer, a thin layer of topsoil thaws for a short time. Lichens, mosses, and some little shrubs cover the tundra. Dandelions and buttercups add splashes of yellow in summer.

The official flower of Nunavut is the purple saxifrage. It can be seen at the feet of the caribou on Nunavut's coat of arms. The purple saxifrage grows low to the ground in gravel and cracks in the rocks. It is usually the first flower to show its purple blossoms in June. The plant forms little cushions or mats. It has small, leathery leaves with tiny, stiff hairs along the edges.

The purple saxifrage was chosen to be Nunavut's official flower on May 1, 2000.

Most of Nunavut is north of the tree line, where it is too cold for forests to grow. In some areas that are sheltered from cold winds, tiny, **stunted** trees grow. The tiny trees that can be found in Nunavut include the dwarf birch, felt-leaf willow, least willow, green alder, and net-veined willow. All of these trees have leaves. None of the trees in Nunavut have needles. Nunavut does not have an official tree.

Common plants such as dandelions grow in Nunavut during the summer months.

The ground in Nunavut is sometimes frozen as deep as 500 metres (1,640 feet).

Some areas of Nunavut get less precipitation than the Sahara Desert.

Inuit use the purple saxifrage flowers to make dye. The petals can also be eaten.

The small trees and tiny plants that grow in Nunavut provide food for animals such as caribou, muskox, and Arctic hare.

Emblems of the Earth

The mainland of Nunavut and Baffin Island are part of the **Canadian Shield**, which contains many minerals. Finding these minerals and getting them out of the ground is difficult because the ground in Nunavut is frozen for most of the year.

There are some mines in Nunavut. Lead and zinc are mined at Nanisivik Mine on Baffin Island. This mine is almost always locked in by ice. Summer is the only time when supplies can be brought to the mine and lead and zinc can be carried out. Miners must be flown in to work at this mine. Mining companies are working on projects to further develop the gold and diamond resources in Nunavut.

Until it closed in 2000, Polaris Mine on Little Cornwallis Island in Nunavut was the world's most northerly mine.

The Lupin Mine on Contwoyto Lake is one of Canada's top five gold mines. This mine can only ship gold out between January and April on temporary winter roads. During these months, Nunavut's lakes and ground are frozen hard enough to take the weight of heavy trucks.

There are large oil and gas deposits in the northern Arctic Ocean. Oil companies are designing the equipment necessary to drill for this oil and gas.

Nunavut does not have an official gemstone or mineral.

Fun Facts

The climate of Nunavut is extreme. Winter temperatures vary over the vast territory, but winter clothing designed for Arctic conditions is necessary at all times. In the summer, mosquitoes can be a problem.

Nunavut is believed to have more natural resources than any other part of Canada.

To make life more enjoyable for the miners, Polaris Mine had a coffee shop, a golf club, and a swimming pool.

A Symbolic Staff

Nunavut has an official mace. A mace is a decorated stick that is carried as a symbol of authority. It represents the power of the territory's government. The mace has been used for centuries in the parliaments of the British Commonwealth. The mace was originally designed to be a weapon to protect kings. Nunavut's mace celebrates the territory's Inuit identity and heritage.

Inuit elders are the keepers of traditional knowledge and the advisors to younger generations. Elders pass on the values and beliefs of the culture to children and youth.

Features

The mace is made of silver and narwhal tusk.

Four silver **loons** intertwine to form the crown at the top of the mace.

Northern jewels and tiny figurines of bearded seals, harp seals, and ring seals are set into the mace. Seals have been an important source of food, hides, and oil for Inuit people.

Carved male and female Inuit figures hold the mace while parliament is in session. These figures represent Nunavut's beginning as the land of the Inuit.

Fun Facts

The Inuit have been making carvings for centuries. They often left small pieces of sculpture behind at campsites as gifts for whoever used the campsite next.

In 2002, Tahera Corporation presented the "Nunavut Stone," a 2.2 carat round-cut diamond, to the people of Nunavut. The diamond will be placed on the mace.

Special Places

Every province and territory has at least one special place that represents its heritage. This place can be a historic site, a monument, a museum, or a park. Nunavut has two important parks—Auyuittuq National Park and Quttinirpaaq (Ellesmere Island) National Park Reserve.

Auyuittuq National Park, or "the land that never melts," was Canada's first national park north of the Arctic Circle. It is located on Baffin Island. Glaciers formed most of the park's landscape of mountains, **fiords**, and deep, U-shaped valleys. The Penny Ice Cap covers 5,100 square kilometres (1,969 square miles) of the 19,500-square-kilometre (7,529-square-mile) Auyuittuq National Park. The Penny Ice Cap formed during the last Ice Age, about 20,000 years ago. It still has ice 300 metres (984 feet) thick in places.

Pangnirtung Fiord is found in Auyuittuq National Park on Baffin Island.

Quttinirpaaq (Ellesmere Island) National Park Reserve is located at the "top of the world" on the northern end of Ellesmere Island. It is Canada's second-largest national park. This park contains the most remote, rugged, and northerly lands in Canada, with high mountains, Arctic tundra, and a polar desert where less rain falls each year than in the Sahara Desert. Ice fields up to 900 metres (2,952 feet) thick still top the mountains in the northern part of the park. This ice is left from the last Ice Age.

Fun Facts

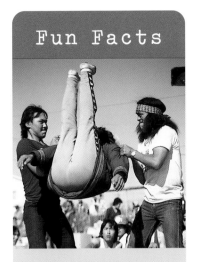

The Northern Games are held every summer. Men and women compete in tests of skills they need to care for a family in Nunavut. Tests include boiling tea, plucking ducks, skinning seals, and making **bannock**.

Inuit actors at Tunooniq Theatre in Pond Inlet use storytelling, drum dancing, and chanting to tell about the past and present life of Inuit people.

Nunavut's rivers and coastal waters offer some of the world's most extraordinary water adventures. People who canoe or kayak in Nunavut must be careful. They could be in danger from cold water, polar bears, sea ice, and walruses.

Quiz

Based on what you have read, see if you can answer the following questions:

1.   What does the qulliq stand for on Nunavut's coat of arms?

2.   Why did the Inuit build inukshuks?

3.   What does the igloo represent on Nunavut's coat of arms?

4.   What does Nunavut mean in Inuktitut?

Auyuittuq National Park Reserve was established in 1976. Auyuittuq became a national park in 2000.

5. Why is the North Star on Nunavut's flag and coat of arms?

6. What is the official gemstone of Nunavut?

7. Which animals are shown on Nunavut's mace?

8. What protects the feet of the Canadian Inuit dog and the rock ptarmigan from the cold?

The Inuit make inukshuks in different shapes and for different uses. They not only provide direction, they also mark places of respect and help the Inuit locate caribou.

Answers

1. Light and the warmth of family and community

2. To guide people and mark special places

3. Inuit's traditional way of life

4. "Our land"

5. The Inuit use the North Star as a guide.

6. There is no official gemstone.

7. Bearded seals, harp seals, loons, and ring seals

8. Fur on the dog and feathers on the rock ptarmigan

Glossary

bannock: traditional flat bread

Canadian Shield: an area of ancient rock that covers part of Canada

fiords: narrow inlets of the sea between cliffs or steep slopes

heritage: something handed down from earlier generations

identity: the qualities that make one person or thing different from all others

latitude: an imaginary line around the Earth parallel to the equator

loons: diving birds that eat fish

narwhals: small Arctic whales

stunted: held back from normal growth

symbols: things that stand for something else

traditional: a custom or way of life that is followed from generation to generation

tundra: a large, treeless plain in the Arctic

Index

Arctic Circle 6, 20
Auyuittuq National Park 20

Baffin Island 5, 16, 20

Canadian Inuit dog 12, 13
coat of arms 8, 9, 14,

flag 10, 11

Inuit 6, 7, 8, 9, 11, 12, 13, 15, 18, 19, 21
Inuktitut 6, 9
Iqaluit 5, 11

mace 18, 19

Northwest Territories 5, 7

Penny Ice Cap 20
purple saxifrage 14, 15

Quttinirpaaq National Park Reserve 20, 21

rock ptarmigan 13